IN SILENCE:
I LISTEN FOR MY POEMS

Derrick S. Slack

Published By
Know Wonder Publishing

www.DSLACK.com

Copyright © 2019 by Derrick S. Slack

ISBN: 978-0-9828657-7-4

OTHER BOOKS BY DERRICK S. SLACK
Know Wonder: A Poetic Journey Through Life Obstacles and Its Wonder ©1998
The Presents of the Beautiful: The Gifts Given by Life and Love ©1999
Whole in My Soul ©2000
P.O.E.M.S. Personal Opportunities to Express Myself Spiritually ©2001
WORLD TOUR: Business for the Independent Artist ©2003
UNLOCKED: Poems I had to breathe...as I exhale ©2004
19,340: The Mountains of Your Dreams ©2010

All rights reserved. No part of this book may be reproduced or transmitted in any form or by any means, electronic or mechanical, including photocopying, recording, or any information storage and retrieval system, without written permission from the copyright owner, except for brief quotations embodied in reviews. All photographs were taken by Derrick S. Slack and are protected under United States and International Copyright laws.

MR. SLACK CAN BE REACHED AT MANAGER@DSLACK.COM; WWW.DSLACK.COM

Know Wonder Publishing is an organization dedicated to the positive pursuits of creativity. Our mission is to Educate, Discover, Develop, and Promote all aspects of creativity and creative endeavors. We Publish all forms of art including, Poetry, Short stories, History, Science Fiction, Painting, Photography, Music, etc. We review all works submitted to us. Please write for any information on publishing with our company.

Printed in the United States of America

First Edition

TABLE OF CONTENTS

	PAGE
In Silence	7
Black Dress	8
O Artista Cubano #1	10
Woman	11
Garden Borders	12
Just Breathe	14
O Artista Cubano #2	15
Beautifully Simple	16
Broken Heart (Part I)	18
Africa	19
Familiar Strangers	20
Hurricane	21
Chillin'	22

Runako's Rain	23
Enoch	26
Ballad of the Brokenhearted: Acid Rain	27
In the Rain	30
Stonewall	31
Piece of History	32
Beauty	33
Numb	34
God Bless Her	35
The Painter	37
Mother: A Great-Grandmother	38
Broken Heart (Part II)	42
Greatness	43
Movement of Mountains	44
Today	46

To my girls: Zyla, Zyon, Zenaya, and any future children I am blessed to have. May God continue to speak to you your dreams, the desires of your hearts, and your gifts to share with this world. I love you and forever will support you.

~Daddy

To my Wife, Taria: thank you for all of your love, care, and support. You inspire me everyday to be a better man. Even though I fall short sometimes, you love me anyway. I will Love you until the day I die.

~D

In Silence….

I hear the wind blowing outside my window and the trees singing, swaying, saying, "I am here, I am alive and I am free." I hear the voice of my mother calling, "Put God first, my son, and everything else will be all right." Have you ever heard the moonlight? It sounds just like the ocean tide ebbing and flowing against the shore. And I am sure that I can hear the sun through its morning glow over the horizon. Thanksgiving dinner. My heart beating. The tapping of the keyboard. Papers shuffling. My pen scratching out a word. I can hear my father's frustration. My family's worry. The story of my people. I hear eyes watching my every move and the knife that is their words stabbing me in the back. I hear my determination and my fears. I hear my tears as they leap from my chin onto the floor. I can hear the door slowly opening and my feet running to meet that opportunity. I hear my past teaching me valuable lessons. I can hear my future through my students. My children's laughter. My loved one's smile. My dreams. My wishes. What do I hear in silence? In silence, I listen for my next poem. For when it is silent — that is when I can hear the voice of God telling me my next poem.

BLACK DRESS

She always looked good in a black dress, he would say as she strutted across the living room floor. "As a matter of fact you look good in anything, baby." She smiled. Not ear-to-ear, but a slight smirk that acknowledged that he was just being nice. You see, each strand of hair had now fallen out; deep, dark circles traced her eyes, her chest ironically swollen from amputated breasts. She looked a mess. And she felt like shit, felt as though she was ready to quit. "Tony, I don't want no funeral, promise me…"

"Baby, you sho do look good in that dress," he said grabbing her hand, kissing it and twirling her around. She smiled again; only this time her tarter-stained teeth shined through her lips.

"I have searched up and I have searched down, and I have found that love is cancer of the heart when you part…" she scribbled in her diary. But deep down she knew that cancer was a question that had no answer and an answer to questions that she wasn't brave enough to ask. She had the task of telling her sons and her daughter that this time she cannot build that bridge over troubled water, and you outta get used to not having me around. But those sounds she could not make, her next breath she had to take, "I'm not through writing my poem," she said. "Dear God, don't let me leave without me finishing my poem."

"You certainly look good today, baby," he told her looking down at her in her hospital gown and dirty wig she wouldn't allow the nurse to take away. This time she cried. Tears flowed down her cheek like raindrops racing to the windowpane. She was in so much pain—the cancer had spread to her brain.

"Tony, I don't want no funeral," she whispered with great effort.

"Baby, what do you mean, you getting outta here soon. You see I brought you your favorite black dress?"

"No funeral, ok, no funeral. Last night, God allowed me to finish my poem. Read it to me, Tony, please read it to me."

Reluctantly, he thumbed through the pages of her journal and found her journey: a photo of her in that black dress, the next 37 pages read, "Please tell me again, please tell me again, please tell me again…."

"Baby you sho look good…in….that…black dress." Wiping the tears away, he pulled the sheet over her head and silently said goodbye.

O Artista Cubano #1

© 2003 Derrick S. Slack HAVANA, CUBA

Havana, Cuba   15 de Mayo 2003

All art is Law. Enforced by an innate spirit that governs peace. Our hearts are bound to a social contract that mandates us to create not for ourselves, but for all. An Artist is the purest socialist.

She is like no other
My mother, grandmother, sister, daughter, wife. She takes
the strife I have in my life and puts a smile on my face where
there once was pain. She's an umbrella in the rain, but she
never blocks out the Son. She works her fingers to the
bone, yet it seems her work is never done.

WOMAN

She is a woman –
She...is a woman!

Gentle like teardrops,
like rainbows, like
water. She is the
daughter of the most high, yet she is grounded like roses
and poinsettias – She has been hurt for centuries, yet hold
no vendettas against the men who want to play with her, but
don't want to marry her, but treat her like a corpse and try to
bury her – But God made her a seed, giving her exactly
what she needs to take root in the very dirt that has been
piled on top of her. There is no stopping her:

She is a woman – She...is a woman

Strong like wind, like a friend, a beautiful child of God, Her
Love does not end. Strong like wind that sends typhoons to
destroy islands, Strong like silence, yet violence can end
with her voice. The strength of her choice can make nations
great – there is no limit to what she can create. There is no
stopping her once she's made up her mind, kind like Ruth,
has the truth of Sojourner, a learner like Mary and Maya.
She has a fire inside of her that is not easily extinguished –
Distinguished like CJ Walker, wealthy like Winfrey, free like
Harriet. The world is often on her shoulders, but with God,
she can carry it. At least that is my experience with the
women God has allowed me to see. She is a force of love
and peace in a world that is often crazed:

*Charm is deceptive, and beauty is fleeting; but a woman
who fears the Lord is to be praised.*

Garden Borders

They said it was a Garden
A Land fertile with opportunity
A place where I could lay the seeds
In my heart and
Pursue the Happiness
Unalienated from my Humanity
They said I could grow here
But I no hear the Freedom Bell
They rang for themselves
For themselves they desire Love
But not for their neighbor
They have sown the seeds of hatred
But no Garden is that sacred
That it should be fertilized with blood
Like this place was

They said it was a Garden
But it seems their empty promises
Do not produce the fruit of the spirit
That they claim they truly believe
But I believe that Eve
Was the scapegoat for the
Disobedience of Man
And they try to justify their inadequacies
By blaming everyone but themselves
But what's the point in believing in God
When we hate the very thing He Loves
Maybe they cannot see God reflected
In anyone else because
They are cousins of the Fallen Angel

And perhaps there is no Garden
There is no fertile opportunity
Where all men were created equal

And endowed by their Creator
With rights that cannot be severed from their nature
And maybe evil has been planted
So deep within this soil
That walls grow where there should be doors
Because the soil has been spoiled
By the seeds of greed, and the illusion of enlightenment
In the form of passionate
patriotism
As if God drew the
borders Himself
You cannot see lines
from space

This place is no Garden

It's a graveyard
Things are put in the ground to die not grow
Watered by the snow
The rain only makes mud
That's why they think we are dirty
They show their love in the strangest ways
But, they actually do love their neighbor
Like they love themselves
Because they *hate* themselves

I pray for the day when we can till the fields
With Justice, Mercy, and Grace
Build bridges of Hope and erase
The pain caused by prejudice and ignorance
Enrich the soil with Joy, Love and Peace
And make it a Garden like they promised in 1776
Intermix with each other to share the Harvest and
Love each other like the God We say we believe in does

Just Breathe

Are you ready for a Revolution?
Are you prepared for a solution?
That moves us from talk to motion
And motion to action
Will we continue to divide our
Faction into fractions
Fractioning our effectiveness
Strangling our struggle
Choking our chances
That make change seem
Impossible
But we can change impossible
Into I'm Possible
Because with faith I'm possible
We are possible
It's now plausible to cause this
Empire to fall
Just breathe
Just breathe like the breath
God breathed when he animated Adam
Humanity has never stopped breathing
Life begins with a breath
Death ends - Just breathe

O Artista Cubano #2

© 2003 Derrick S. Slack OLD HAVANA, CUBA

Old Havana, Cuba 15 de Mayo 2003

All art is War. Its very nature is protest. Continual overt oppression cannot erase its power. It is created because of our circumstances — and in spite of them. It seeks controversy and demands attention. It destroys complacency, rendering culture.

Beautifully Simple
(In Memory of Ricaldo Machado)

In the early morning, as sun was rising just over the horizon in Trinidad, he looked into her eyes and with a boyish grin asked, "do you remember me?" And it was then they spoke, laughed and joked and talked about all that their minds could think of. And even when they ran out of things to say, they would sit and stare at each other, because even the silence was as loud as the sunrise, and just as beautiful. God was prescribing to them happiness, and joy always comes in the morning. It was the dawning of a new day.

And she smiled as he commanded her attention and ever so often he would mention, "I never want to let you go." So by midday they were married, telling her, "I will carry with me your heart so that I will never be alone." He wanted her forever by his side until the day God called him Home.

In the afternoon they had children, Nigel, Shelly, Rodney and Rhonda proclaiming to the world, "Let no man put asunder what God had united." For He has lighted their course and forced the dimness of gloom to never consume their day.

Love is so beautifully simple: they argued and disagreed, and worked, and laughed and talked, went shopping, played, prayed and stayed in each others arms watching television, ate dinner together, walked to the kitchen, mixed ideas, never mixing friendship and poker, spoke on the phone, joked with the children, rested, traveled, cut the grass, bought cars, took pictures, became grandparents, and apparently they found time to build a home together, weathering all the storms that life blew their way.

"I'm solid as a rock, strong as ten men and never run second." He beckoned the forces of God to give him strength as dusk was beginning to steal the light from his vibrant body that once graced soccer fields and drove sports cars. But his shortness of breath would sometimes make simple tasks very difficult.

And soon the sun was setting, the moon was near and life was calling it a day. But needless to say, he wasn't going to retire into the night with out a fight. Besides, as long as he had her he had a reason to want to see the sun again. So often he pulled her close and cried out that she be there when he was afraid to sleep, afraid to give up hope, afraid that his body was just too weak to undergo any more test or procedures. And she proceeded to be there for him, giving him everything that he needed, just to make life more simple again.

But inevitably the day had to come to a close, for not even the mighty sun can fight forever the ending of the day. So now his fight was over and he lives where there is no darkness, only the peaceful and beautifully simple memories they shared in Love.

And when her day comes to an end and the sunsets take her away from us, she will join him in the Kingdom of God. And as the sun rises just over the horizon, she will look him in the eye and with a girlish grin ask, "do you remember me?" And they will laugh and joke and talk again forever …

Broken Heart (Part I)

I know you have a broken heart
I know your heart is broken
But a broken heart can only be broken
If it once has experienced love
And a heart that has felt love
Is one that has lived
And a heart that has lived
Is one that has seen beauty
And beauty is the active ingredient of peace
And love does not cease
Even with a broken heart
Even when you are apart
Even when you're lost and don't know what to do
Love is an epoxy that epitomizes power
That sticks you to memories like glue
Strong is enough to make you weak
Just weak enough that anyone can have it
And when you have it –
it somehow makes you strong…

Africa

Sometimes I see her standing in my dreams
        She seems to be whispering and I cannot hear her
        Still I listen
        The sound seems to glisten off the rain
That pours from her cheek
        I seek to find her standing in my dreams
        And she seems to be reaching out for me
                She does not touch me
                Yet I know she can feel me
        Still I want to touch her
        I need her to touch me
If only it is her words that caress my skin
        As we begin to end the past
Of broken hearts and pursue a future
        unkown

©2004 Derrick S. Slack   Cape Coast, Ghana

FAMILIAR STRANGERS

We are not strangers
    Even though we have never met
        We are twins
            And share a Mother that gave
    Birth to us
On separate continents…

H U R R I C A N E

She came into my life like Hurricane Ivan
And I've been waiting for her for such a long time it seems
Why do hurricanes form so far away at sea
At a place where one cannot see to assess its potential damage
And this one is slowly approaching my coastline
Beckoning destruction
Begging the question *Should I evacuate?*
Or should I brace myself and stay
And weather the storm she brings my way
I don't want to board up my windows
Or bolt down my doors
But I have put so much time and energy into building my Home
So is it enough to merely hope that she will shield me with her eye
Protecting me from the fierce winds that surround her
Compound her, abound her
Astounding she is to me
Which proves the dilemma
A wise man once told me
The only difference between genius and stupidity is in the
outcome
How come we must wait so long
For the determination of whether
we need to wear a poncho all day
Or whether I should bring a raincoat to the beach just in case
Even so, how can I truly enjoy the sunshine
When I feel rain is imminent
And clouds are no longer beautiful
But potential storms
Such is life
And I have lived long enough to know
That weathermen are not always right
But more importantly
Storms usually come to an end
But still, I need you to understand
I have permanent scars
From the last storm that blow my way

©2004 Derrick S. Slack   ITURE, GHANA

C H I L L I N '

RUNAKO'S RAIN
(in Memory of Runako Chioke Flax, died in Atlantic Ocean, 26 August 2004)

Loneliness surrounds us
Like the night sky with no stars
Raindrops descend like teardrops from Heaven—
God cries through clouds
Loud like thunder
Each drop seeps under soil trapping sunlight
As the flowers bloom
Where God cries it is always Beautiful

And I've seen those tears before
In the eyes of a Mother as they
Stream down her face like a river
Searching for the sea
Trying to see if she can make it past this emotion
Wondering why God had to cry an ocean
That swallowed her son
Like he was an ancestor in transition
This transcendental beauty
Only God can explain, but
Where God cries is it always Beautiful

And I've seen those tears before
The water in a daughter's eyes cries, asking
"Where is my Daddy, is he coming home soon?"
Yes child just look into the moon or
Catch a Sunbeam as you sit by the windowpane
Remember his smile and it will ease your pain
He belongs to the water so dance in the rain
And run through those puddles
And when your eyes flood with tears
It's just him wanting to cuddle

Joy always comes after the darkness
Which is usually at dawn
And if you go out onto the lawn
You too can know this to be true
When you touch the morning dew
Or inhale the humidity after a storm
And feel its warmth
That cures the cold loneliness he left us
Like the night sky without any stars

So I am asking, begging
Lord, open your clouds and cry for us
You see, I want it to rain
Rain for my Mother
So she can feel her Son shine again
So she can hear his voice whispering
Through the hallowing wind
Make the rain touch her hand
So she won't have to rely so much on
Photographs to find his fingertips
Make it rain so she won't have to pour so many
Tears into her rubber plant
Make it rain so the echoes left over from hand written letters
Won't flood her blood with pain
Make it rain so hard that she remembers her Sunbeam
Has returned to the vapors

I now know why weeping willow trees
Are found near the water
So it can continually cry for a daughter
Who has lost her Father
And God will make it rain for her too
Only this time it will sound like music from the piano
Feel like hugs from Grandma
And look like the kind of tears that

Come from laughing too hard
Because after God cries Rainbows appear
Lakes are seen on the distant horizon
Ocean are replenished, thirsts are quenched, and flowers bloom
There's no way we can live without those tears

So wherever there is water we ought to
Give thanks and praise to the Most High
Because where He cries
Life is certainly more Beautiful

© 2004 Derrick S. Slack   Elmina, Ghana

ENOCH
(dedicated to Enoch Mensah—Ghana, West Africa)

Enoch thinks he can fly
And I believe him
Believe in him and the possibilities of rising high
He wants to fly not as birds do
As they spread their wings and glide upon the wind
But he wants to ascend like men
Who dream of life greater then themselves
He needs help though
So he sits by the shore to ensure
The spirits hear his heart beating through the sound of his drum
Calling on the forces of God to deliver a way
To enflame the internal burning fire
That is fueled by his desire to rise higher
Than what one would think is possible for
Someone like him
But for someone like him
It would be more impossible to fail
Because when you try you will prevail
Assail upon the limitless skies
Fly like a successful interview
Fly like "I can do anything, be somebody"
Fly like, "I will let nobody stand in my way"
Fly like a prayer being answered
Like learning something new
Like going to school
Like confidence being restored
Fly like ignorance being ignored and education embraced
Fly like a dream turning into reality
Like a dream becoming reality

Enoch thinks he can fly
And I believe he knows it
I pray God will show him how
Medase African one, *Medase*
Thank you Enoch for showing us your wings

Ballad of the Brokenhearted: Acid Rain

Who is going to fight for the dancing girl?
When her face has lost its beauty
When she is showered in shame
Shown that we just don't care
Who will stand up for her right for existence?
What specific provision
Can we provide for her condition?
So that when she dances, she moves
To the beat of a difference drum

Little girl, why were you born
If all you are going to do is die
When was it you decided that your life
Was not worth living
Living to dance in the streets
With strangers each night
Intertwining and soaking your soul in sin
No One will fight for you
Because you're a whore
And whores are useless
After we use them
We suck the life out of you
And then curse you for being dead
No one will hear your tears
Because you cry with an accent we disdain
Your pain is something we cannot feel
We stab you with indifference
And tell you that your pain isn't real
You see we dance to different songs
Even though the lyrics are all the same
Yours seems to be sung all wrong
Yours sing with too much shame

Who is going to fight for the dancing girl?
Who is going to tell her she is lovely in spite of...?
Who will tell her that she is the light of
A darkened soul, that she is pure gold
That her beauty is in the beholder's eye
That when she cries, her tears
Have the potential to water character
Tell her that her heart is covered in fertile soil
It only seems dirty, because she has planted seeds
Of sadness and sorrow
No one has told her that she could
Borrow hope from tomorrow
That God can repair her wounds
No one has told her the her
Beauty is NOT skin deep!

I cannot hate you
For in doing so will perhaps
Damn my daughters to a destiny
Of destructive dancing
I cannot rebuke the Devil in them
And wish it in you
For you belong to a wider Sisterhood
A network of God's most precious treasures
Of which my girls are a part
That is why I tell them each day that they are smart
And encourage them to dance with their Father
Whose Love will be a canopy covering them
From the acid rain
That will heal them of any pain
And convince them that their
Beauty is already obtained
So daughter of a distance Land
You need not be ashamed
God will ensure that you will never be alone

Your right to live is not predicated
On the places you call home

Who will fight for the dancing girl?
I will because she is my sister, daughter
My lover, friend, mother and wife
Because her life is valuable
I will fight
And we both can learn
To dance to the beat
Of a different drum

*Dancing Girl = Prostitute

Dedicated to all acid attack victims worldwide, know that you are beautiful, human, and deserving of our love and respect

...In The Rain

Can't you see I'm caught in the rain? Shivering, slowly excepting this hypothermia. I never knew I needed to ask the sun to deliver its warmth. Things just came easy for me, so forgive me if I expect my day to have Sunshine. But I realize the moon has always been a contestant in control for my happiness. And yes, the darkness has a sizable lead. It appears that I am smiling, but that's only because my world is upside-down. Living my paradox has taught me a few things: it's always cold in the morning, and chances are it may not stay that way. So again, forgive me if I pack an extra blazer, Mama told me expect the worse and be surprised — it's better than being disappointed. So here I am in the rain, standing before a mountain — boots laced and gear in place, preparing to climb.

Stonewall

(Part I)

The President
The epitome of the bootstrapper
Humble, first generation anything
Rude, brash, unapolgetic
A war hero
That's why our borders extend
Far beyond the reaches of the Mississippi
And the Chicktow, Cherokee, and Creek
Creep into historical oblivion
The tears still trail
The Frontier's trials still traverse a course
That cannot be reversed
The wounds yet to be healed by time
Florida's acquisition bears witness
To the power he wielded
And Spain's claim to the Native Land
Had to be relinquished
I have no praise
For the trauma still persists

© 2000 Derrick S. Slack   NEW YORK CITY, USA

Pictures are a piece of History. Places in our persona we go to and remember happy times. Beautiful memories of friends we don't see anymore and Locations we no longer visit. We only look upon them as reminders of what once was, of who we once were.

And we often smile, longing to relive those moments once again. And maybe that is wonderful that we cannot see that time again because of who and where we are.

But maybe we are saddened by those memories because of the utter joy we have recorded on the Photographic Page of our History...

BEAUTY (for Dountonia)

Summers filled with laughter – The backyard was a jungle
A graveyard to Ziggy – You may have forgotten to feed him
The front yard was an isolated world:
Fun-filled adventures – it was there was found Beauty
The aroma of cakes and chicken,
Baked tenderly, carefully seasoned,
Mama used to make the macaroni and cheese right
-     Three cheeses and a lot of Love   -
Homemade rolls and Popsicle stains
On the no-wax kitchen floor,
Every flavor but orange – you didn't like orange
Family visits from Aunt Kay, Aunt Sue,
Sometimes Uncle John who lived down the street
DD was a live
His brown hat rested on the porch next to the coffee
can, filled with no formal education, yet a lot of
knowledge - to us it was just tobacco juice,
It was there we found Beauty
Fouth of July tents,
Sounds of card games and trash talk,
Bar-B-Que smells invaded the neighborhood
Beauty's bold chlorophyll provided a shaded comfort
78 degrees in her presence, the mercury told us 83
Swinging from her branches
She witnessed the dangerous gashes of growing up,
And innocent disputes of siblings
And the Spin-the-Bottle birthdays
Her beautiful branches became a means
To correct our mischievous behavior,
It even hurt when we left her.
And now she stands there
Missiing the innocence of yesterday
And the orchestra of Life we harmonized
In our childhood.
She just stands there unchanged
Calling us back to the Beauty that we once knew

N U M B

It's been a long time coming
           Love fades like the summer sun
         Disappearing into the horizon
       And it's surprising
           That evermore can turn into not ever again
And then to add insult to injury
I made you lose your energy for loving me
          And I'm not saying it's all my fault
       But I do take the blame
              And I will burden the shame
            I wanted you to have my last name
          But too little too late is the song you sang
Each time I brought you my heart on a platter
         But now it doesn't really matter
              Whether or not love is splattered
        Like paint upon your soul's canvas
     I just need you to translate love
      Into my heart as if it were Spanish
And love is a loquacious language
That lifts you from the lagoon of sorrow
          Into the warm waters of the sea
            It is he sight you seek as you walk blindly in caves
          It protects you from tidal waves
It takes away your liberty
        Placing you in total submission to its touch
         It makes too much not enough
            Maybe this is too much for you to handle
              And just like the candle
          In the open window waiting for the inevitable
           No matter how incredible the flame
            One slight breeze can blow it silent
Just as the violent winds we have woven into
The fabric of our friendship
Our souls become mute   Our hearts deaf
        And our hands are numb
        Because we just can't feel anymore

GOD BLESS HER

She's beautiful
I saw the sun rising in Her eyes and
A fruited plain and purple mountain
And I sighed,
I cried because I couldn't believe
That something this beautiful
Could treat me so unpleasant
Like a peasant I am in Her presence
The essence of nothing
She says I am just more
than half a man
She may never understand
who I truly am
But that has never stopped me from
loving Her
From giving Her my all
Standing tall in the face of adversity
Shielding Her from perversity
From injury I fought and protected
But She neglected me with misery
She told me history will repeat
Itself if I am not careful
Oh, but I am cautious
Because I know that true
Reciprocity is fictitious
That is why I am suspicious
Each time She smiles at me
Whispering softly
"Everything will be all right"
Blinded by Her beauty,
I feel that what She's saying is true
Everything will be all right

God bless Her
She's beautiful
If you've ever inhaled the ocean air at dawn
Smelled a summer day of a freshly cut lawn
If you have ever seen a blue jay or a cardinal
The artful display of geese in formation
Flying South to where it is warm
Then you have been in Her arms
That is the Freedom She speaks of
When She is holding you
She makes you believe in possibilities again
At least I do
And all I need her to do is place Her
Hand across Her heart and say
"I pledge allegiance to you too"
But I can never get Her to commit
Or submit to Her truest feelings
So those words may remain unspoken
And though my heart is broken
I will continue to Love Her
Because love is supposed to be unconditional
And just maybe Her hurting me is unintentional
From what She was taught by Her Fathers
And why bother arguing with Her

About things in our past we both cannot change
So I look forward to the future
The day She is loving and accepting me for
What and who I truly am—a Man

The Painter

You've searched
But I found you
Jigged with colors
As the canvas
Caresses my eye.

I want to dance
With you once again
In the midst of
Your Creativity

You are covert
In your approach
But it is obvious
What you are
Trying to do

You are calculating
In your escape and
I find you jigged
With colors, dancing
Like brushstrokes
Against my Soul.

Mother: A Great-Grandmother

Mother was mean
And not the kind of mean that means average
The kind that when she spoke
She said exactly what she meant
The truth was never bent
She gave it to you straight up
With no filter, no screen
It wasn't meant to be mean
If she saw green she called it green
You know what I mean?

And she would tell you if you were ugly too

And I can respect that

She was a great Grandmother
Not because her daughter had a daughter
Who had a daughter
But because she provided water
For our soul to sip on when it thirst
Because she put her family first
Because when times were at its worst
She was there with a smile
That simply stated:
"Stop your daggone whining, look how far I've made it,
I have lived a great life
There's no way I'd trade it
So there is no need to complain
Plant your seeds in fertile soil
They will only grow with the rain"

Somehow sunshine would follow her
Happiness would tag along for the ride
Wherever she went joy was by her side
And when a smile wouldn't work
She carried a knife in her pocketbook
Give you look that could launch a thousand ships
You never knew what would escape her lips
And that not only made her unique
It also made her beautiful
Suitable to sit with God in Heaven
If God were to grant her one more day
Mother would take eleven

Because she did her own thing
Like she had her own song to sing
Walked as if she had her own theme tune
She Lived 52,326,720 minutes
Yet why does it seem she was taken away too soon
She sitting in Heaven right now
Probably watching wrestling
Or sorting through her Goodwill clothes
Happiness now will eternally surround her
No more sorrow no more woes
So I know she would not want us to be saddened
She held the patent on personality
And in reality
She would be upset if we were to cry
Hang our heads and sigh
She would be wondering why

Why we aren't partying
She left this world so that she could be our guardian
So let's celebrate her Good life
Not be distraught at her death

She has taken enough breaths
For all of us combined
Lived a full life
Left a wonderful legacy behind
There is always a tendency at these
Gatherings to say something kind
But in this case at least we can mean it
For we all have witnessed her love
We have lived it and we have seen it
We have all been blessed to have been
In her presence
Feeling her effervescent beauty
That seemed to be everlasting
And no we should not be masking our pain
But at least we should be perpetuating our pleasure
For this beautiful treasure
That we have known as a Great Grandmother

And she wasn't a great Grandmother
Simply because her son had a son
Who had a son
It was because she was our sun
And she would shine bright as the stars would at night
Gave us light on the darkest days
Made us feel special in multiple ways
And yes I will miss those days
Where I can see her
And to always have her near
But if she did anything right
Then we all should have a piece of her here
And we should realize that in us
She will always be near

Dedicated to Louise "Mother" Slack 1917-2017

Broken Heart (Part II)

Love is also why we hope
Love is the reason we must cope
Press on and continue to move forward
And look forward to the day that
We can meet our family and friends again
Because life does not end when it ends
Because when it ends
There is a beginning
There is a "so long, friend, I'll see you later"
Love is an equalizer and an equator
Love is an elevator
Elevating us to a higher place
Even in the face of unimaginable pain
Love is the anesthetic that soothes
Our broken heart like an umbrella in the rain
Love is the gift that keeps on giving
So what we must do is keep on living
Living each day as though it was our last
Remember the past, yet prepare for tomorrow
Take our sorrow and turn it into sun rays
So that it will no longer darken our hearts
But give us brighter days

Greatness

I refuse to take my greatness to the grave
Or be a slave to my fears
I will steer my dreams not just follow
I will swallow my pride and risk it all
All because I am destined for greatness
Greatness that I will magnify
Not justify complacency
And through all the obstacles facing me
I will chart a course among the stars
Because that is where I belong

©2004 Derrick S. Slack   Elmina, Ghana

The Movement of Mountains

I can move mountains. I can push them aside to see the horizon skies and take in the beautiful view of limitless possibilities. Or climb to its summit, submitting to my dreams, accomplishing my goals, being the pot of gold at the end of rainbows. I am valuable. I know I am worth more than the reasons why this is impossible, and there isn't anything I will not pay to prove to myself of what I am capable.

I can move mountains. With my mind molded around positive thoughts like armor that shields me from the destructive forces of "I can't," "You will never," "You're not smart enough," "You're not old enough," "You're too old," "Not bold," "People like you don't," "You won't," "You couldn't," "You shouldn't," "You can't!" But I can. I am ready for the challenges that lie ahead and even those in which appear invisible. I have vision. And though I am sometimes blind-sided by blinding thoughts of negativity I can use the corrective lenses of hard work and self-determination to make my dreams reality.

I can move the highest mountains. Overcome the utmost resistance. Pursue the peaks of pessimism that erupt to try and kill my spirit. I can carve out a caldera with my consciousness simply because I believe I can. And with God I am even much more than what I think I am.

And you — you can move mountains. You can. I've seen you. I have seen you move through the mountainous monotony that monopolizes your moments of joy. I have seen you scale the cliffs of insecurity and hike the hillsides of hunger to find happiness. You move mountains through your students, through your children and your babies. I have read them in your books on the pages of your pursuits and passion. You have traveled to the highest heights even as family members were lost; you found time to share your gifts. You move mountains through your smile. You climb with your convictions. You jump from peak to peak effortlessly but still remain humble enough to be surprised at your accomplishments. People like you create schools, improve communities, instill values, dare to dream, overcome obstacles, assail adversity, change the world, move mountains.

You can move mountains. I can move mountains. We move these mountains so that we can show others how they can move their own.

©2006 Derrick Slack, Mt. Kilimanjaro, Tanzania

Today

Today is the first day I start Living
I will capture my Freedom by being giving
I will accept the role that I was meant to be
Will accept the challenge of being just me
I will Dream with change as my intention
Give Freedom and life my fullest attention
I will be that voice with the capacity to dare
Show my fellow brethren the utmost care
I will listen twice as much as I speak
The Journey of Love I will boldly seek
I will be that being that represents light
Use my heart as my only sight
Use my mind to mold my existence
Pursuing to learn with care and persistence
Today is the first day that I am me
And today, I am FREE.

www.ingramcontent.com/pod-product-compliance
Lightning Source LLC
Chambersburg PA
CBHW071650040426
42452CB00009B/1822